P9-BYH-249

ATLANTIS
AND OTHER LOST WORLDS

By John Hawkins

PowerKiDS
press
New York

Published in 2012 by The Rosen Publishing Group, Inc.
29 East 21st Street, New York, NY 10010

Author: John Hawkins
Editor and Picture Researcher: Joe Harris
U.S. Editor: Kara Murray
Design: Emma Randall
Cover Design: Emma Randall

Picture Credits:
Bill Stoneham: 22. Corbis: 4, 10, 12, 16, 29. Frank Joseph: 8, 9, 15, 17, 19, 20, 21, 32. Shutterstock: cover, 1, 5, 6, 7, 11, 14, 18, 25, 26, 27, 28. TopFoto: 24.

Library of Congress Cataloging-in-Publication Data

Hawkins, John.
 Atlantis and other lost worlds / by John Hawkins.
     p. cm. — (Mystery hunters)
 Includes index.
 ISBN 978-1-4488-6429-4 (library binding) — ISBN 978-1-4488-6441-6 (pbk.) —
ISBN 978-1-4488-6442-3 (6-pack)
 1. Atlantis (Legendary place)—Juvenile literature. I. Title.
 GN751.H32 2012
 001.94—dc23

                            2011021292

Printed in China
SL002063US

CPSIA Compliance Information: Batch #AW2102PK: For Further Information contact Rosen Publishing, New York, New York at 1-800-237-9932

CONTENTS

WHAT WAS ATLANTIS?

According to legend, Atlantis was a beautiful, rich, and powerful island nation. It was described by the ancient Greek philosopher Plato in about 360 BC as lying "beyond the Pillars of Heracles" (the Straits of Gibraltar). However, according to Plato, in the middle of a war between Atlantis and Mediterranean countries in 9000 BC, the island sank into the sea in a single day and night.

▲ This is an artist's impression of the architecture of Atlantis, with a great temple rising above the rest of the city.

IMPERIAL CITY

According to Plato, the island of Atlantis was mountainous and lushly forested. South of Mount Atlas, its towering dormant volcano, was a fertile plain irrigated by a network of canals. South of the plain was the city of Atlantis, capital of a mighty oceanic empire.

The city of Atlantis, Plato records, was composed of circles within circles of land and water connected by bridged canals. Each artificial island was surrounded by high walls and mighty watchtowers.

▲ *Plato claimed that the citizens of Atlantis worshipped the sea god Poseidon.*

sea god. The kings had absolute power over their cities and regions. However, they accepted the judgement of the other rulers on any complaint made against them. Poseidon's laws forbade the kings from making war on each other and required them to take united action against any external enemy.

The smallest central island contained the imperial palace and magnificent temple of the sea god Poseidon, legendary founder of Atlantis.

RULERS OF ATLANTIS

Plato explains that the empire was governed by ten kings, all directly descended from the

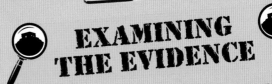

EXAMINING THE EVIDENCE

DID ATLANTIS EXIST?

The legend of Atlantis has been a source of fascination ever since it was rediscovered by scholars in the 17th century. But did the island ever actually exist? Atlantologists (seekers of Atlantis) argue that a large landmass may once have existed in the location of the Mid-Atlantic Ridge. The Ridge certainly suffers from earthquakes and volcanoes. However, most Plato scholars believe that his Atlantis was imaginary. Plato's story could have been inspired by the fate of the island of Santorini in the Mediterranean. Santorini was destroyed by a volcanic eruption in about 1600 BC.

WHAT WAS LEMURIA?

Lemuria, or Mu, is a lost island said to have existed long ago in the Pacific Ocean. In 1864, zoologist Philip Sclater realized that fossils of lemurs were found on Madagascar (an island off Africa) as well as India. He proposed that both countries were once part of a larger continent, which he named Lemuria.

PACIFIC CULTURE

The idea of the lost continent of Lemuria was picked up by nineteenth-century believers in supernatural phenomena, such as Helena Blavatsky, William Scott-Elliot, and James Bramwell. According to their theories, Mu was a culture that spread its influence over many Pacific islands before it was swallowed up by the ocean. Forced to abandon their homes, the Lemurians settled in Melanesia and Polynesia. Some moved to Central and South America.

▼ Could the monumental sculpted heads of the Olmecs in Mexico have been influenced by Lemurian culture?

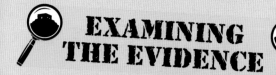
DID LEMURIA EXIST?

The mainstream scientific community no longer believes that Lemuria existed. According to the theory of plate tectonics, accepted now by all geologists, Madagascar and India were indeed once part of the same landmass, but plate movement caused India to break away millions of years ago and move to its present location. The original landmass very slowly broke apart. It did not sink beneath the sea.

▼ According to some, the statues of Easter Island are evidence of the existence of Lemuria.

SPIRITUAL EMPIRE

Blavatsky and her colleagues believed that Mu existed at the same time as Atlantis. However, they said, the two civilizations were very different. While Atlantis was a technologically advanced and warlike culture, the Lemurians were a simple, seafaring people. They sailed to other parts of the world to spread their spiritual beliefs. They built ceremonial centers, sacred sculptures, and roads. Mu's influence, they said, can be seen in statues such as the colossi of Easter Island.

SEEKERS OF ATLANTIS

Following the collapse of ancient Greek and Roman civilization, Plato's story of Atlantis was dismissed and forgotten. However, this story of a lost island was revived in the seventeenth century by the German Jesuit priest Athanasius Kircher.

KIRCHER'S MAP

Kircher was the first scholar to seriously study the Atlantis legend. His research led him to the immense collection of ancient sources at the Vatican Library. Here he came across a well-preserved leather map of Atlantis. The map had come to Rome from Egypt in the first century AD, but Kircher believed it had been made in the fourth century BC, during Plato's time. The map shows Atlantis as a large island. It shows a high, centrally located volcano, most likely representing Mount Atlas, along with six major rivers.

▲ This map of Atlantis was found in the Vatican Library by Athanasius Kircher. Does it show a real place?

RUDBECK

Olaus Rudbeck (1630–1702) was a Swedish professor of medicine and amateur archaeologist who found evidence for Atlantis through

▲ *U.S. Congressman Ignatius Donnelly was adamant in his belief that Atlantis really existed.*

DONNELLY AND BERLITZ

The man most responsible for bringing Atlantis to the attention of the wider public was Ignatius Donnelly (1831–1901), a U.S. Congressman and founder of Atlantology. Donnelly's 1882 book, *Atlantis, the Antediluvian World,* was a runaway bestseller and is still published in more than a dozen languages. The work of popularizing Atlantis was later taken up by Charles Berlitz (1913–2003). A talented linguist, Berlitz concluded that many modern and ancient languages derive from a single prehistoric source, which he argued could be traced to Atlantis.

excavations and research in his own country. He claimed that Norse myths and archaeological evidence proved that some survivors from Atlantis had come to Sweden. Their influence, he said, led to the rise of the Vikings.

EYEWITNESS TO MYSTERY
IMMORTAL PINNACLES
The poet William Blake (1757–1827) was inspired by the legend of Atlantis to write: "On those vast shady hills between America and Albion's shore, Now barr'd out by the Atlantic sea, call'd Atlantean hills, Because from their bright summits you may pass to the Golden World, An ancient palace, archetype of mighty Emperies, Rears its immortal pinnacles. . . ."

TECHNOLOGY OF ATLANTIS

According to Atlantologists, the great, lost civilization was incredibly technologically advanced. The citizens of Atlantis, so Atlantologists claim, mastered flight many millennia before the invention of the plane by the Wright brothers.

▲ Could the flying temples of the Hindu scriptures have been inspired by real Atlantean technology?

ANCIENT AVIATORS?

At the end of the nineteenth century, an ancient wooden artifact that looked exactly like a model airplane was excavated in the Upper Nile Valley. Ancient Hindu sources refer to aircraft called Vimanas. The Incas told stories of an age-old hero called Kon-Tiki Viracocha who rose high into the air aboard a flying temple. In southwestern North America, the Hopi Indians spoke of Pauwvotas, airborne vehicles flown over immense distances by an ancestral people before their island perished during the Great Deluge. Atlantologists theorize that these folk memories are all that remain of a lost Atlantean supertechnology that created some kind of aircraft.

BUILDERS AND MINERS

One area in which Atlantologists believe the Atlanteans excelled was building. The Great Pyramid is the oldest of the Egyptian pyramids.

From whom did the Egyptians acquire these building skills? The Egyptians record that Thaut, survivor of the flood that brought his fellow "followers of Horus" to the Nile Delta, was the Great Pyramid's chief architect.

The Mnemonie Indians of North America's Upper Great Lakes region tell of the marine men, white-skinned people from across the Atlantic who dug out Mother Earth's shiny bones. This is a reference to copper miners who excavated between 3100 BC and 1200 BC. The miners used "magical stones," which the Indians called Yuwipi, to locate the underground veins of copper. Could the pale-faced foreigners have been Atlanteans using their mining skills in North America?

▼ Some authors have claimed that the pyramids were built by Atlanteans to transform seismic energy into electricity.

HOW WERE ATLANTIS AND LEMURIA DESTROYED?

The French astronomer G. R. Corli was the first person to conclude, in 1785, that Atlantis was destroyed by a comet colliding with the Earth. Dismissed at the time, the idea was revived in the 1930s by Austrian engineer Hans Hoerbiger, who blamed the impact of a fragment of frozen comet for the catastrophe. In 1964, German engineer Otto Muck found twin deep-sea holes in the Atlantic floor. He claimed these were caused by an asteroid that set off a chain reaction of subsurface volcanoes along the Mid-Atlantic Ridge.

▼ It would have taken a truly huge disaster to obliterate Atlantis so completely.

ATLANTIS—COMETS AND ASTEROIDS

Atlantologists point to two major cometary impacts that could have destroyed Atlantis. The first was in about 2200 BC and the second in 1198 BC. This seems to agree with historical records. Plato and the Roman scholar Varo wrote of floods occurring around 2200 BC. The Chinese myth of ten suns falling from the sky has also been dated to around the twenty-second century BC.

Atlantologists believe that Atlantis may have survived the 2200 BC disaster, but that its final end came with the bigger catastrophe of 1198 BC, which brought an end to the Bronze Age.

Geologists estimate that asteroids struck the eastern North Atlantic in that year, with global effects. This is reflected in writings of the time.

LEMURIA—VOLCANOES AND TSUNAMIS

A series of geological upheavals appear to have brought great destruction to the Pacific during the late seventeenth century BC. At that time, Japan's Mount Sanbe and Alaska's Mount Aniakchak erupted, spewing ash into the atmosphere. During the same period, Rabaul in the South Pacific and Hawaii's Mauna Kea exploded. Could the combined effects of these eruptions have been sufficient to destroy Lemuria?

STRANGE STORIES
"The waves uprose"
Polynesian myth recalls the destruction of Marae Renga, a legendary "land of the Sun." "Uvoke lifted the land with his crowbar. The waves uprose, the country became small. . . . The waves broke, the wind blew, rain fell, thunder roared. . . . The king saw that the land had sunk in the sea." Hotu Matua, who led survivors to Easter Island, lamented, "The sea has come up and drowned all people in Marae Renga."

LEGACY OF ATLANTIS: NORTH AFRICA AND EUROPE

In about 3100 BC, Egypt began its swift rise from a simple farming society to a sophisticated civilization that built temples, developed a written language, and excelled in science, engineering, and the arts. Atlantologists have argued that this transformation came about due to the arrival of Atlantean refugees in the Nile Valley, following the destruction of their homeland.

PAINTINGS AND MYTHS

Atlantologists offer different kinds of evidence to support this argument. For example they point to the Egyptian myth of Thaut. Thaut, it is said, arrived in Egypt at the dawn of their civilization bearing tablets of knowledge. He was fleeing a flood that overwhelmed his homeland.

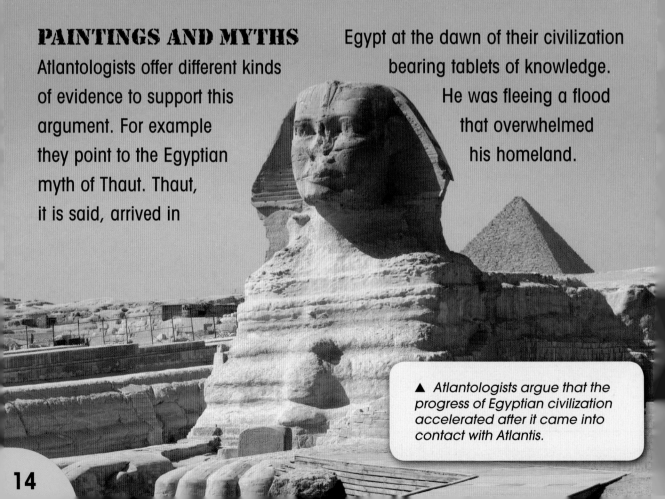

▲ Atlantologists argue that the progress of Egyptian civilization accelerated after it came into contact with Atlantis.

▲ *Some writers have claimed that the man in this Egyptian ceramic is an Atlantean prisoner.*

described Atlantis. Could there have been a wave of immigration from Atlantis to Spain?

BASQUES

Further north, the Basques of the Pyrenees speak of their prehistoric forefathers as inhabitants of Atlaintika. They were said to have sailed from the "Green Isle," a powerful seafaring nation that sank into the Atlantic. The Basque language, Euskara, is unrelated to any Indo-European tongue, but shares similarities with the language of the Guanches, natives of the Canary Islands, and Nahuatl, the language of the Aztecs. All this, Atlantologists say, suggests a link to Atlantean culture.

FLIGHT TO SPAIN

Near the southern Spanish city of Jaén are the remains of an ancient city laid out in concentric circles of canals and land rings, just as Plato

STRANGE STORIES
Dog worshippers

The Canary Islands got their name from the Romans because of their custom of dog worship. "Canis" is Latin for "dog." Atlantologists see a link between this and the ancient Egyptian cult of Anubis, the dog-headed god. Both peoples, according to Atlantologists, were descended from the Atlanteans.

LEGACY OF ATLANTIS: THE AMERICAS

As with the Egyptians, the rise of civilization in Central America was swift, with the emergence of the Olmecs in about 1250 BC. Atlantologists believe Atlanteans and Lemurians may have helped in the development of Olmec culture.

MAYA AND AZTECS

According to Mayan tradition, the Maya's first city, Mayapan, was founded by Chumael-Ah-Canule, the "First after the Flood." He escaped the Hun Yecil, the "drowning of the trees," that engulfed his island kingdom across the Atlantic Ocean. The temple frieze at the Mayan city of Tikal begins with the image of a man rowing his boat away from an island city tumbling into the sea during a volcanic eruption. The Aztecs, a later culture, claimed ancestral descent

▼ *Was the architecture of Tikal influenced by Atlantean ideas?*

▲ *This Chibchan Indian artwork shows the "Gilded Man," their founding father who arrived from across the sea. Some claim that he was a survivor of Atlantis.*

commemoration of the Great Flood. Mandans paint their skin white to mimic their ancestors who arrived from across the Atlantic.

from the lost volcanic island kingdom of Aztlan in the Atlantic Ocean.

NORTH AMERICA

Tribal myths also seem to point to a lost Atlantean heritage. The O-kee-pa ceremony of the Mandan Indians in the Dakotas is an annual

According to James Churchward, a writer on the Mu, evidence of a Lemurian presence in North America can be found in the Hopi sand paintings of swastikas. This hooked cross, known in Buddhism as the sauvastika, is a common image in Asia. Churchward believed that both the Asians and ancient Americans may have received this symbol from a common source, Lemuria.

STRANGE STORIES

Tales from South America

The indigenous peoples of South America have myths that seem to fit in with the Atlantean legend. The Chibchans of Colombia tell of their founder Muyscas-Zuhe, who came from an island in the Atlantic after it was overwhelmed by a great flood. The Ge-speaking Indians of Brazil speak of the king Mai-Ra, who set his island on fire, then sank it beneath the sea, because of its people's immoral conduct. He then sailed to South America with a small band of companions chosen for their virtue.

THE SEARCH FOR ATLANTIS: THE NORTHEAST ATLANTIC

In 1949, Dr. Maurice Ewing, aboard the research vessel *Glomar Challenger*, found an ocean-floor formation in the Northeast Atlantic, later dubbed the Horseshoe Seamounts. It was made up of a large mound ringed by a range of mountains. Its highest peak was a volcano that had collapsed beneath the sea in the past 12,000 years. Could this have been the large island surrounded by a ring of mountains described by Plato?

▼ According to Plato's writings, "There was (on the island of Atlantis) every kind of animal, domesticated and wild, among them numerous elephants."

▲ *This map show the ocean floor in the Atlantic. Off the coast of Portugal can be seen a ring of mountains matching Plato's description of Atlantis.*

to tie in with Plato's story that these creatures had inhabited Atlantis.

In 1974, cameras aboard the Soviet research vessel, *Academician Petrovsky*, captured a series of images resembling the partial remains of human-made ruins. Most appeared around the peak of Mount Ampere, around 213 feet (65 m) below the surface.

BEACH SAND AND ELEPHANT BONES

Expeditions to the undersea mound have retrieved freshwater sand, algae, and rocks that had been formed on dry land, all of which suggested that it had once been an island. Even elephant bones have been dredged from the area, seeming

? FACT HUNTER

THE HORSESHOE SEAMOUNTS

Could this be the site of Atlantis? The island's estimated dimensions seem similar to those given by Plato. Mount Ampere stands to the south, the same position assumed by Mount Atlas in Plato's description.

So why hasn't Atlantis been found yet? If a ruined city does exist on Mount Ampere, it will be under many layers of silt, mud, and possibly lava rock. No device currently available is capable of penetrating such thickly layered obstacles.

And if we do penetrate the silt, what will we find? Probably very little. Even if Atlantis is down there, the cataclysm that destroyed it, if powerful enough to sink an entire island, is unlikely to have left much in the way of cultural evidence.

THE SEARCH FOR ATLANTIS: THE CARIBBEAN

▼ A deep-sea submarine equipped with state-of-the-art equipment dives into the seas around Bimini in search of evidence of Atlantis.

In March 2003, amateur explorers Greg and Lora Little were snorkeling off the island of Andros in the Caribbean when they came across what appeared to be a giant underwater platform made of three tiers of massive stone blocks.

ANDROS PLATFORM

The platform was 1,502 feet (458 m) long and 164 feet (50 m) wide. Its regular appearance and square-cut blocks suggested it could have been a dock or port of some kind. But what ancient civilization could have built such a massive structure at a time when the area now covered by ocean was dry land? Over the following years, more discoveries were made in the area, including a long stone wall 6 miles (10 km) north of the island. Atlantologists believe this could have been a western outpost of the Atlantean Empire.

BIMINI ROAD

The Bimini Road is an underwater rock formation near the island of Bimini in

Road to the ancient wall of Lixus on the Atlantic coast of Morocco, which is made of huge blocks of square, unmortared stone perfectly fitted together. They argue that the two structures were made by the same Atlantean civilization.

▲ *Atlantis researcher Vonda Osman with a block of stone removed from the Bimini Wall.*

the Bahamas. The structure is made up of huge square blocks that run in two straight lines across the sea bottom for about 2,083 feet (635 m). The road contains what appear to be several angular keystones with notches to join them together. This is similar to a prehistoric building style encountered in the Andean walls of Cuzco and Machu Picchu. Atlantologists also compared the Bimini

EXAMINING THE EVIDENCE
IS THE BIMINI ROAD NATURAL OR HUMAN-MADE?

Most conventional geologists believe the Bimini Road is a natural feature composed of beachrock that has broken up into a variety of shaped blocks. They say it is a peculiar result of natural processes that can also be found in other parts of the world, including the Tessellated Pavement at Eaglehawk Neck, Tasmania. Atlantologists dispute this. They say that at the time of its formation, it stood well above sea level, so no wave erosion was possible. They also point to samples revealing fragments of granite, which is not found in the Bahamas.

THE SEARCH FOR LEMURIA

In 1985, a Japanese scuba instructor was diving in the waters off Yonaguni, an island in Japan's Okinawa island chain. The diver found himself facing what appeared to be a great stone building. The photographs he took of the structure sparked national interest. Archaeologists examined the photographs, but could not agree if the structure was natural or human-made.

▼ This is an artist's rendering of the sunken monument lying in the waters off the Japanese island of Yonaguni.

UNDERWATER CITY?

The following year, another diver in Okinawa waters was shocked to discover what looked like a massive underwater arch, perhaps a gateway, of huge stone blocks. They were beautifully fitted together in the manner of prehistoric masonry. This sparked another surge of interest, and by the autumn of 1986, five more apparently man-made structures were found near three Japanese islands. The formations seemed to be made up of paved streets and crossroads, altar-like formations, grand staircases leading to broad plazas, and processional ways surmounted by pairs of towering features resembling pylons. So far, no internal passages or chambers have been found.

If these structures are man-made, who could have built them? Some people claim these are the remains of the lost world of Lemuria. The Lemurians, they say, were either overwhelmed by rising sea levels or the land on which they built these structures gradually collapsed.

SPIRAL STAIRCASE

In 1998, divers found yet another seemingly human-made underwater ruin near the islet of Okinoshima, over 600 miles (966 km) from Okinawa. It was a row of four round stone towers, each one 23 to 33 feet (7–10 m) across and almost 100 feet (30 m) high. One of them featured a spiral staircase winding around its exterior.

EYEWITNESS TO MYSTERY
DESCRIBING OKINOSHIMA
Professor Nobuhiro Yoshida says, "Comparing these linear steps, so perfectly suited to anyone climbing them, with the immediate subsurface environment, we notice at once that the sea bottom is otherwise composed exclusively of irregular, round boulders. . . and therefore in sharp contrast to the vertical columns and rising staircase."

LOST WORLDS OF THE AMERICAS

Atlantis and Lemuria may be humankind's most famous lost civilizations, but there are other phantom realms that play powerful roles in the mythology of different peoples. The lure of these fabled worlds, and the riches they may contain, have tempted many explorers to try and find them.

EL DORADO

Invading Spaniards in the early sixteenth century observed Colombia's Chibchan Indians practicing the Guatavita ceremony. This ceremony was in honor of their forefather, a legendary golden king. The Spanish convinced themselves the king's city, El Dorado, still existed somewhere in the Colombian interior, and they spent several fruitless centuries searching for it.

▲ The Spanish conquistador Coronado mounted an expedition in search of the legendary Seven Cities, but they forever eluded his grasp.

SEVEN CITIES OF GOLD

In 1150 AD, as the Moors besieged the city of Mérida in Spain, seven bishops and their congregations fled across the Atlantic by ship. It was rumored they landed on another continent where they built seven cities, rich in gold and precious stones.

the seven caves," and the Spanish immediately interpreted that to mean Cíbola. Unfortunately for them, the legendary seven cities were never found.

▲ A ceremonial Colombian gold mask. European explorers became convinced that the city of El Dorado contained countless such treasures.

The legend of Cíbola, as the seven cities became known, persisted, and when the Spanish conquered Mexico in 1519, they were eager to find it. The Aztec emperor Moctezuma II told them of a place to the north called Chicomoztoc, meaning "place of

CITY OF THE CAESARS

A myth tells that ancient Roman sailors, fleeing civil unrest following Julius Caesar's assassination, were shipwrecked on the southern tip of South America. The story went that the Romans used their expertise to build the Incas an extensive road network, and the native population was so grateful they showered them with gold, silver, and diamonds. The Romans then went on to build a fabulously wealthy city in Patagonia.

STRANGE STORIES
Did the Romans really reach South America?
The City of the Caesars was never found, but some intriguing discoveries have been made that suggest the Romans may well have reached South America. From a shipwreck found off Rio de Janeiro, Brazil, in 1976, Roman amphorae were retrieved, identified by an expert as dating from around 250 AD. Bricks used to build the Maya city of Comalcalco were found to be stamped with second-century AD Roman mason marks.

LOST WORLDS OF THE NORTH

The icy northern regions of the Earth have always exerted a fascination on people, both ancient and modern, and they have often been the subject of rumor and myth.

▲ *Thule was associated by the ancient Greeks with the aurora borealis, the Northern Lights.*

HYPERBOREA

In Greek mythology, Hyperborea, meaning "beyond the north wind," was a mythical land existing far to the north. In this perfect place, the Greeks said, the sun shone for 24 hours a day. In this they were not far from the truth. Beyond the Arctic Circle, the sun does shine for 24 hours a day for half the year, between the vernal and autumnal equinoxes. According to the ancient Greeks, the Hyperboreans were sun worshippers. Some modern researchers have speculated that Hyperborea could have in fact been Great Britain. The description of the Hyperboreans' great temple seems similar to Stonehenge.

THULE

Another mysterious Arctic realm is Thule, supposedly visited by the

▼ *The great temple of Hyperborea supposedly resembled Stonehenge, the prehistoric monument near Salisbury, England.*

ancient Greek explorer Pytheas in the fourth century BC. Pytheas recorded that Thule was a six-day sail north of Britain and was near the "frozen sea." Later, classical writers placed Thule to the northwest of Britain and Ireland, beyond the Faroes, which means that Thule could only have been Iceland. But if so, who were the inhabitants that Pytheas claimed to have found there? Pytheas described them as farming people, producing grain, fruit, dairy products, and honey.

Yet, according to conventional history, Iceland was not settled until the Vikings arrived there in the ninth century AD.

? FACT HUNTER

STONEHENGE

What is it? It's a prehistoric monument in southern England, composed of earthworks surrounding a circular setting of large standing stones.

When was it built? Most archaeologists believe the stones were erected between 3000 BC and 2200 BC.

What was it used for? The culture that built it left no written records. However, scholars have speculated that it was used as an astronomical center or as a religious site for sun worshippers, possibly the Hyperboreans.

SHAMBHALA

▼ *Shambhala, if it exists, is a place of beauty and tranquility.*

Shambhala is a mythical kingdom in the Tibetan Buddhist tradition. It is often associated with Shangri-La, but the latter is a fictional place, invented by British author James Hilton in his 1933 novel *Lost Horizon*. "Shambhala" is a Sanskrit term meaning "place of peaceful happiness." It came to be regarded as a perfect place hidden in a Himalayan valley.

NOT A PHYSICAL PLACE?

Shambhala has been located at various sacred sites in or near Tibet, including the capital, Lhasa, and Potala, the former residence of the Tibetan spiritual leader, the Dalai Lama. However, His Holiness the 14th Dalai Lama said that Shambhala is not a physical place, but somewhere that can only be arrived at through spiritual enlightenment.

HUNZA

This has not prevented people from seeking Shambhala. In the 1920s, two Russian expeditions tried and failed to find it. Some believed it to be Hunza, a thousand-year-old principality in northern Pakistan. This remote and verdant valley was said to have been populated by a mainly Buddhist community, which spread its influence to nearby Kashmir.

▼ Shangri-La, in China's Yunan Province is a tourist destination named after the fictional paradise of James Hilton's novel.

AGARTHA

Others have linked Shambhala to Agartha, another mythical kingdom located underground. Agartha is apparently lit by its own subterranean sun and populated by people 13 feet (4 m) tall who will one day fulfill an ancient prophecy by establishing their divine leader as king of the world.

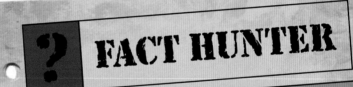

? FACT HUNTER

SHANGRI-LA

What is it? In James Hilton's novel, Shangri-La was a mystical, harmonious valley located in the Kunlun Mountains.

What is its significance? Shangri-La has come to be used as a term for any earthly paradise or permanently happy land, isolated from the outside world.

What is its connection to Shambhala? Hilton was inspired by stories of Shambhala, which was being sought by Eastern and Western explorers at the time he wrote his novel. Shangri-La literally means "Shang (a region of Tibet) Mountain Pass".

GLOSSARY

Albion (AL-bee-on) A poetic term for Britain or England.

amphorae (am-FOR-ay) Tall ancient Greek or Roman jars with two handles and a narrow neck.

archaeologist (ahr-kee-AH-luh-jist) A scholar of human history and prehistory through the excavation of sites and analysis of artifacts and other physical remains.

artifact (AR-tih-fakt) An object made by a human being, typically something of cultural or historical interest.

asteroid (AS-teh-royd) A small rocky body orbiting the Sun. A few enter the Earth's atmosphere as meteors.

Atlantologist (at-lan-TAH-leh-jist) A seeker of lost worlds, particularly Atlantis.

cataclysm (KAT-ah-cli-sum) A large-scale violent event in the natural world.

ceremonial center (ser-ih-MOH-nee-ul SEN-tur) A place where formal events of a religious or public nature are carried out.

comet (KAH-mit) A celestial object consisting of a nucleus of ice and dust and, when near the sun, a 'tail' of gas and dust particles.

concentric (kon-CEN-tryk) Describing circles or other shapes that share the same center, the larger ones surrounding the smaller.

earthworks (URTH-werks) A large artificial bank of soil.

equinox (EH-kwih-noks) The time of the year when day and night are of equal length. There are two equinoxes each year, the vernal (spring) equinox and the autumnal (autumn) equinox.

frieze (FREEZ) A broad horizontal band of sculpted or painted decoration.

geologist (jee-AH-luh-jist) A scientist who studies the Earth's physical structure and substance, its history, and the processes that act on it.

Heracles (HER-ah-cleez) A Greek hero of superhuman strength who performed twelve immense tasks.

irrigated (IR-uh-gayt-ed) Supplied with water by means of channels.

Jesuit (JEH-shyoo-wit) A member of the Society of Jesus, a Roman Catholic order of priests founded in 1534 to do missionary work.

keystone (KEE-stohn) A central stone in a structure, which locks the whole thing together.

linear (LIH-nee-er) Arranged in a straight line.

linguist (LING-gwist) A person skilled in foreign languages.

Neolithic (nee-oh-LI-thik) Relating to the later part of the Stone Age.

Nile delta (NYL DEL-tuh) The triangular-shaped mouth of the Nile River where it diverges into several outlets.

pagan (PAY-gun) Relating to beliefs other than those of the main world religions.

principality (prin-suh-PAL-ih-tee) A state ruled by a prince.

pylon (PY-lon) A monumental gateway of an Egyptian temple, made up of two tapering towers.

skeptic (SKEP-tik) A person inclined to question or doubt the opinions of others.

subterranean (sub-tur-RAY-ni-an) Beneath the Earth's surface.

FURTHER READING

Kallen, Stuart A. *Mysterious Encounters: Atlantis*. Farmington Hills, MI: Greenhaven Press, 2011.

Linnéa, Sharon. *Lost Civilizations*. New York: Sterling, 2009.

Martin, Michael. *Atlantis*. Mankato, MN: Capstone, 2007.

Shone, Robert. *Atlantis and Other Lost Cities*. New York: Rosen Publishing, 2006.

WEB SITES

Due to the changing nature of Internet links, PowerKids Press has developed an online list of Web sites related to the subject of this book. This site is updated regularly. Please use this link to access the list:

www.powerkidslinks.com/mysthunt/atlantis/

INDEX